A Healthy Life

BY CHELSEA KONG

© 2021 Chelsea Kong

All rights reserved. All images used in this book are licensed copies from their respectful owners including Freepik. This book or any portion thereof may not be reproduced or used in any manner whatsoever without the express written permission of the publisher except for the use of brief quotations in a book review.

Printed in 2021, Made in Toronto, Canada
ISBN: 978-1-7775796-7-8
Library and Archives Canada

Please make sure to get a copy of
A Healthy Life book to use this workbook.

Just to say thanks, you can get a free book here:
https://chelseak532002550.wordpress.com/books-for-sharing/

Dear friend, I pray that you may enjoy good health and that all may go well with you, even as your soul is getting along well. (3 John 1:2)

God's will is for us to live in good health.

Learn to rest and how many hours to work.

Make the right choices.

EAT WELL

A healthy life is the best life for us.

Our food today is missing most of what we need to eat.

Vitamins and minerals and pure clean water that have been restored are important.

Eat well, drink well, and live well.

HEALTHY LIFE IN THE BIBLE

God gave them water to drink.

Seeds and nuts were good for food.

No animals were eaten.

WHAT HAPPENED?

Adam and Eve disobeyed God and He killed an animal and clothed them.

Animals were used to give an offering to God.

Cain and Abel were both farmers, but out of jealousy Cain killed Abel because he gave God the best offering.

NOAH

God told Noah to build an Ark because people did evil in His eyes and wanted to destroy them.

After the flood, God told Noah and his family that they can eat meat.

Noah gave an offering to God.

FOOD LIMITS

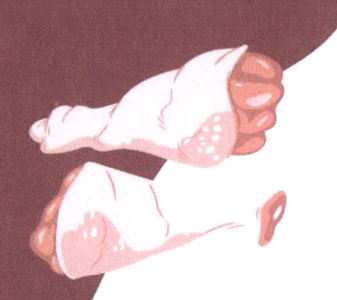

God told His people what food they can eat and what they should not eat.

They can eat any animal with the divided hoof and chews the cud.

Avoid eating food with blood in it.

You can eat food with fins and scales.

BIRDS

There are different birds that we should not eat (Leviticus 11:13-19).

The birds we are not to eat are unclean in God's eyes.

We can eat chicken, duck, goose, quail, and some others.

BUGS

Some flying insects that walk on all fours that you may eat.

Those that have jointed legs for hopping on the ground.

Some bugs are locusts, katydid, cricket, or grasshopper.

UNCLEAN ANIMALS

Animals that crawl on the ground
are not clean to eat.

The weasel, the rat, any kind of great lizard,
the gecko, the monitor lizard, the wall lizard,
the skink, and the chameleon.

Be aware of rats in the home as they like
to eat any food left on the ground or open.

MEATS, FISH, AND SEAFOOD

The best meat to eat for food:

Beef from Cows

Chicken

Fish and Seafood (Salmon is the best)

Turkey

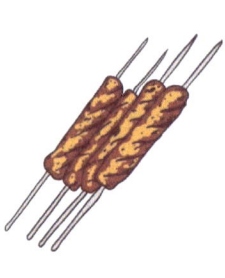

OTHER MEATS

Veal

Lamb

Buffalo

Goat

Venison (Deer)

BEST VEGETABLES

Potatoes, Sweet Potatoes, Yam, Taro, Squash, Pumpkin.

Carrots

Broccoli

Mushrooms

Green Leafy Vegetables like Spinach, Kale, and Brussel Sprouts.

OTHER VEGETABLES

Beets

Garlic and Ginger

Green Peas, Beans, and Collard Greens.

Asparagus

Kohlrabi

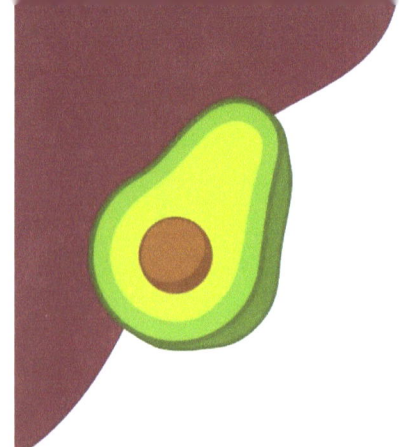

FRUITS

Grapefruit, Oranges

Pineapple

Avocado

Blueberries, Strawberries, Cranberries, Rosehip, Blackberries.

Apples

OTHER FRUITS

Pomegranate

Mango

Lemons

Banana

Olives

MORE FRUITS

Grapes

Watermelon

Guava

Papaya

Cherries

Still more!

NATURAL SWEET FOODS

Honey

Stevia

Sugarcane

Maple Syrup (from the Tree)

GRAINS

Whole wheat made from Einkorn grain.
Rice (non-gluten)

Oats

Quinoa

Millet

NUTS

Almonds

Walnuts

Pistachios

Cashews

OTHER NUTS

Pecans

Macedemia

Brazil

Hazelnuts

Peanuts

SEEDS

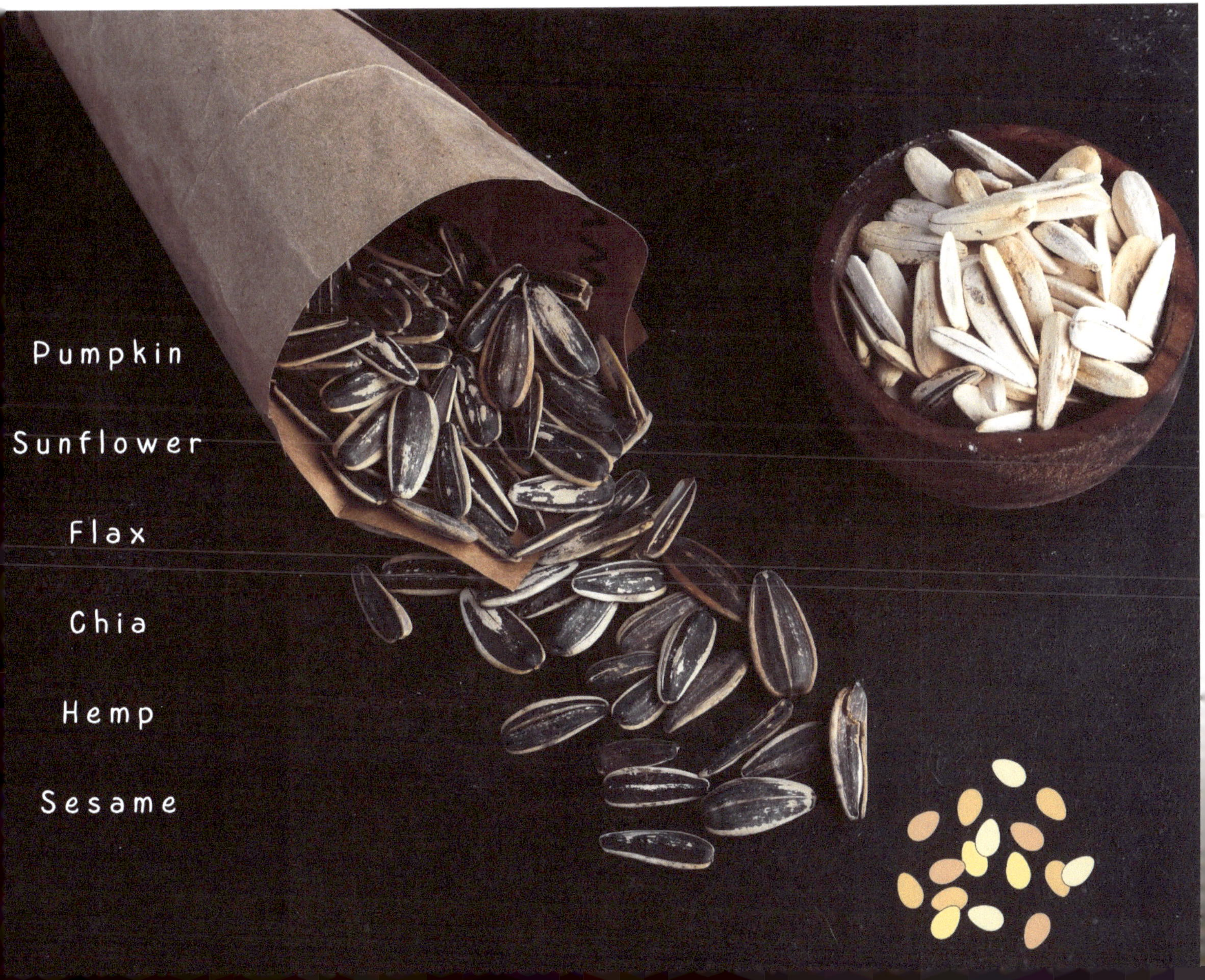

Pumpkin

Sunflower

Flax

Chia

Hemp

Sesame

DAIRY AND NON-DAIRY FOODS

Cheese

Milk

Yogurt

Butter

Almond Milk, Coconut Milk, an Soy Milk.

JUICES

Fresh-made juice is the best without sugar added.

Vegetable Juices

Fruit Juices

Coconut Juice

SMOOTHIES

Smoothies with whole milk

Vegetable smoothies

Fruit smoothies

You can mix milk, fruits, and vegetables.

WATER

We need the right number of cups of water to drink.

We need pure clean water that has what we need for our body (vitamins and minerals are needed).

Natural spring water

Reverse Osmosis water

Alkaline water

TEAS

Pine Needles

Green

Black (Oolong)

White

Jasmine

HERBAL TEAS

umpkin

nflower

Flax

Chia

Hemp

Sesame

OTHER HERBAL TEAS

Rooibos

Sage

Lemon balm

Rose Hip

Passionflower

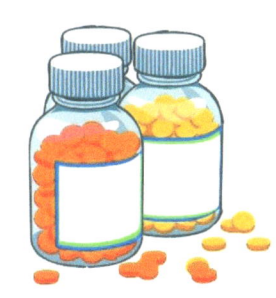

VITAMINS AND MINERALS

There are vitamin and supplement tablets, pills, capsules, and powder (soft is better for our health).

Minerals also can come in powder, a drink, and other.

The more natural they are the better.

Check for high in milligrams (mg) and grams (g).

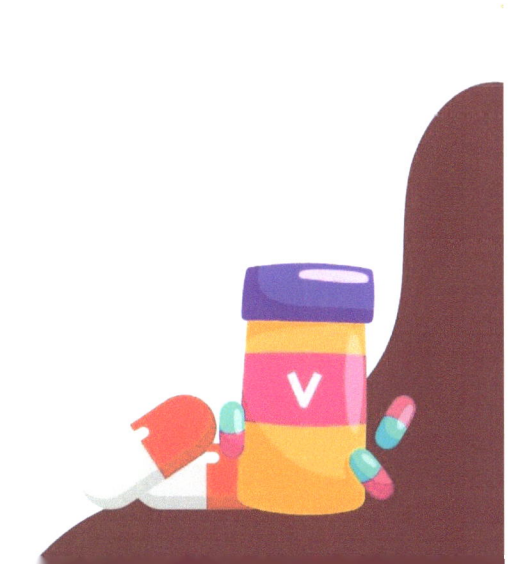

TYPES OF VITAMINS

Vitamin A

Vitamin B1, B2, B3, B5, B6, B7/8, B9, B12.

Vitamin C

Vitamin D

Vitamin E

Vitamin K

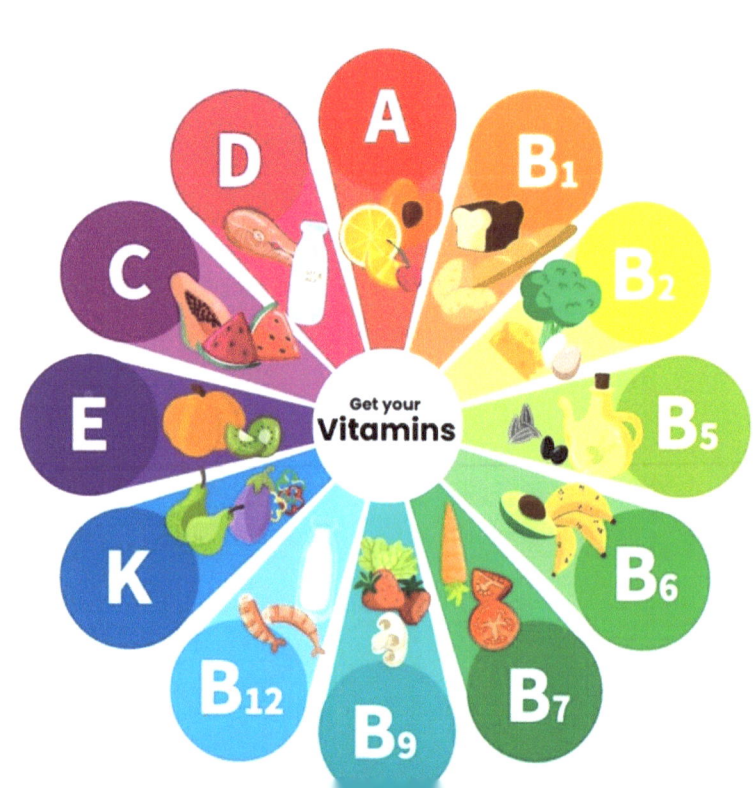

MINERALS AND MORE

There are 60 different minerals that our body needs.

There are 12 amino acids and two essential fatty acids.

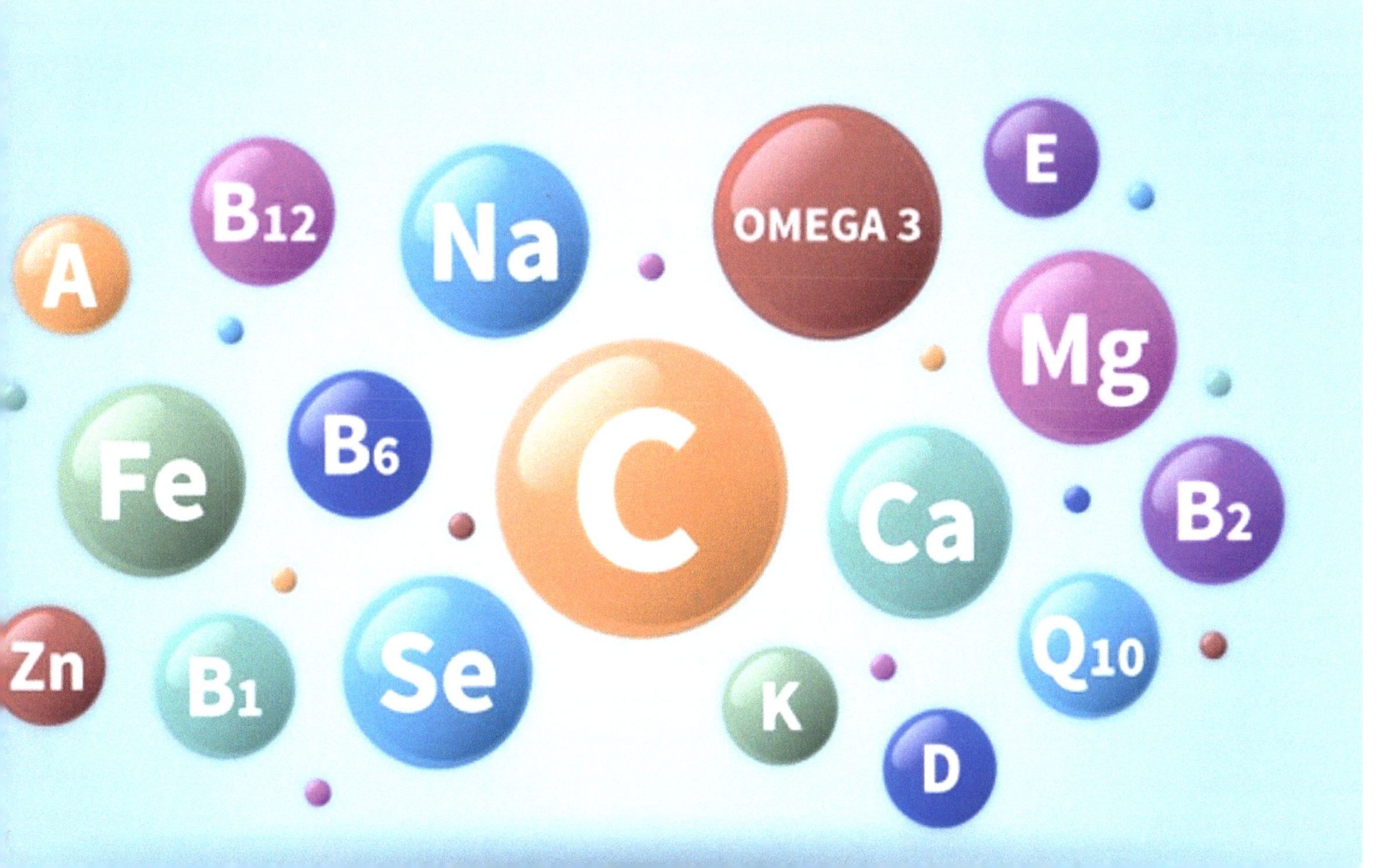

MINERALS AND MORE

Dr. Joel Wallach is a famous doctor that has learned and helped many people to become healthy.

When we eat all these 90 essentials, we will be healthy.

All sickness and disease can be gone by eating right.

SUNLIGHT

We need to have 15 minutes of sunlight several of times each week.

It gives the body Vitamin D.

The sun gives 10,000 IU to 20,000 IU of Vitamin D in 30 minutes.

You can also buy vitamins and minerals with high IU.

EXERCISE

We need to exercise every day for at least 15 minutes.

There are many sports you can do outside.

You can also take a walk, run, or go hiking.

You can also do exercise inside like dancing.

SLEEP

We need to have enough hours of sleep every day.

Most people need 8 hours of sleep, but some need 6.

Sleep is good for our body, brain, feelings, soul, and to be strong.

It gives us energy every day to do everything and lets the body rest (our liver must have rest)

PRAY

Pray every day to keep close to God.

You need to know Him, Jesus, and Holy Spirit.

Pray also in the words God gives you by the Holy Spirit (secret talk that keeps the evil away).

Pray God's Word

Pray for others.

GOD'S WORD

Know His Word and what it means.

Learn how to live in peace, love, joy, and more.

Read His Word every day and three times a day.

Speak The Bible verses out loud and believe in Him.

SALVATION PRAYER

God, I know I sinned against you. Forgive me for the wrong that I have done. I believe that Jesus Christ died on the cross for me. That He rose from the grave after three days so that I can have His long-lasting life. Come into my heart to be my Lord and Savior. I choose to turn away from my sins and I choose to follow you. Lead me to walk with you. Keep me safe and teach me your ways. Stop every bad thing in my life that has an open door to hurt me. Close those doors. Holy Spirit fill me now in Jesus' name. Amen.

BAPTISM IN THE HOLY SPIRIT

Jesus, you are the one that fills me with Your Spirit. Come Holy Spirit and come into my life and fill me to overflow with Your presence. Come with your fire too. Thank you for the gift of tongues in Jesus' name. Amen.

BAPTISM IN THE HOLY SPIRIT

Open your mouth and let the words come out that God gives you. It will be words that you don't know what they mean. You can ask God what it means. You need to let Him talk through you every day to grow this gift. He will bring you closer to God and you will know Jesus more. You will have power from God to do great things and know things.

 # PRAYER

Father, teach me how to eat healthily and live a healthy life. That I can also drink right too. Remind me of what your word says. That I will have enough sun, water, and exercise. That I also will have enough of what my body needs. Teach me also how to avoid food that is not healthy in Jesus' name. Amen.

MESSAGE FROM THE AUTHOR

God's plan is for us to live a long life. He knows what we need. We need to ask Him and we will have more than enough every day. He can bring us to places where we get the highest milligrams and grams of vitamins and minerals. Our body likes to eat other food that is not good for us if we are not careful. It must be taught to eat right all the time. Anything that is not organic and original food is bad for us. The best tea is leaf teas. You can make your tea too. Dandelion leaf and root tea and also eat Spirulina (seaweed) too. No GMO also is better for health.

OTHER PRODUCTS

- Knowing God
- How to Hear God's Voice
- New Life in Jesus
- Loving Israel
- God's Gifts
- Meeting God
- Word Power
- Fruit of the Spirit
- The Tabernacle
- Bride for Jesus
- A Life of Prayer
- Live Free
- Who am I in Jesus
- Walk in Love
- God's Favor
- Man of God
- Woman of God
- How to Use Money
- God's Wisdom
- Fasting
- See Jerusalem and Bethany
- First Fruit Offering
- Feast of Trumpets
- Day of Atonement
- Feast of Tabernacles

- Counting the Omer
- Festival of Lights
- Glory, Presence, and Holy Spirit
- Live in God's Presence
- 31 Day Devotional
- Biblical Puzzle Book Vol 1
- Biblical Puzzle Book Vol 2
- Biblical Puzzle Book Vol 3
- Biblical Puzzle Book Vol 4
- Biblical Puzzle Book Vol 5
- Bible Puzzles for Young Children Book 1
- Bible Puzzles for Young Children Book 2
- Bible Puzzles for Young Children Book 3
- Biblical Puzzle for Children Books 1-3
- How God Speaks
- Knowing Jesus
- Knowing Holy Spirit

OTHER PRODUCTS

Teaching Series

How to Hear God's Voice Teaching Guide & Audio Book

Relationship with God, Jesus, Holy Spirit Guide

Knowing God, Jesus, Holy Spirit Guide & Audio Book

Teaching (Non-Sale)

Purim

Passover

Resurrection

More books to come!

More books on Amazon, Kobo, and Barnes and Noble
https://chelseak532002550.wordpress.com/

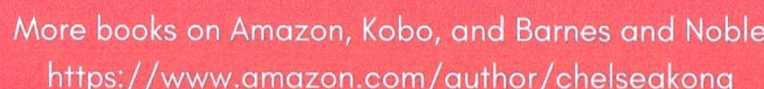

More books on Amazon, Kobo, and Barnes and Noble
https://www.amazon.com/author/chelseakong

Please leave a review to help the author continue to write more books to reach more readers. Thank you so much for your support.

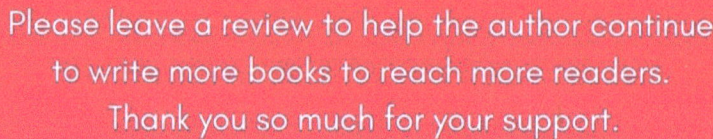

A HEALTHY LIFE WORK BOOK

There are other healthy foods not mentioned in this book that you might find that are also very beneficial. At the time of writing, I compiled as many as possible and the best that I could find without it being too long for children to read. You can also check for A Healthy Life Work Book to go with this book.

Leave a review on Amazon!

About
CHELSEA KONG

She is a writer, creative arts and digital media artist, skilled administration professional, and podcaster. Chelsea also served in a variety of roles, from audiovisual, photography, to assisting on the worship team, and ministry team. She also has a passion for families being united.

Chelsea graduated from Hotel and Restaurant Management, Digital Media Arts, Office Administration, and experience working with children. She mainly writes children's books, stories, bridal writing, poems, lyrics for songs, words of encouragement, blessings, prayers, and jokes. The author of How to Hear the Voice of God, the Bridal Collection, Knowing God, etc. She also has her own Bible Puzzle books and other inspired products. Her podcast channel is called Chelsea K on Anchor, Spotify, and iTunes. She has been on Unity Live Radio and The Lady Tracey Show and is highly recommended by a Proud Christian blog.

Please check my website to find out more:
https://chelseak532002550.wordpress.com/

REFERENCES

Wallach, Joel, Dr. "The 90 Essential Nutrients." The Wallach Revolution, 2015, https://thewallachrevolution.com/

Biblegateway, NIV, ICB. N/A, https://www.biblegateway.com/

www.ingramcontent.com/pod-product-compliance
Lightning Source LLC
Chambersburg PA
CBHW041413010526
44107CB00016B/1155